T0064502

You Don't Know Anything About a Woman Until There Are Mice

Wisdom and Advice Gone Awry

Earl Humphrey

authorHOUSE®

AuthorHouse™
1663 Liberty Drive
Bloomington, IN 47403
www.authorhouse.com
Phone: 1-800-839-8640

Published by AuthorHouse   07/13/2015

ISBN: 978-1-4969-1647-1 (sc)
ISBN: 978-1-4969-1646-4 (e)

Print information available on the last page.

About the Author

Earl Humphrey does his writing from of a home office that is built on a bluff, where he writes on the same principal. Throughout his personal and professional life, Earl was constantly the recipient of conventional wisdom and advice from the ever-present "They" (as in "You know what They say ..."), whether he asked for it or not. He patiently took in all this wisdom until he had had enough and decided to strike back and give "They" some wisdom of his own. "They" should be very worried.

Earl is a Professional Disruptor and darn proud of it. While living in Los Angeles, he was the Executive Producer and CMO of the award-winning Blue Beetle children's educational videos. He has studied, performed, and written improv/sketch comedy with groups at the Comedy Workshop in Houston and ImprovBoston in Boston. Earl takes great pride in inflicting the world with the type of twisted wisdom that people cannot get out of their heads and then makes them laugh at inappropriate times. He regularly inflicts the world with his special kind of wisdom on his website: www.earlhumphrey.com

Earl lives with his wife Mary on a small farm near Delavan, Wisconsin. He is frequently seen on his antique Ford 9N tractor plowing fields for no apparent reason.

Contents

Preface

I dedicate this book to those who wish they had said some of these things and those who sleep better knowing they did not.

With all the questionable advice we are bombarded with every waking moment of our lives, someone had to step up to the plate and start making nonsense of it all. And that someone is me.

For years, I've written down on scraps of paper and in notebooks gems of wisdom, clichés, and advice I have heard or have been given. A few years ago, I started putting all these into one notebook.

From that notebook came the seed of the idea for this book.

If any of you out there have actually said any of these things, I promise not to publically give you credit for your lack of taste and prudence.

Prepare to be haunted by some of the most irrelevant things that have never been said—until now.

I have suffered from others' wisdom, and now it's time for them to suffer from mine.

Let the lack of wisdom begin.

Section 1

Taking Wisdom Down a Couple Notches

It's a rare person who keeps a stash of extra batteries.

When you hear the word "culture," remember where you came from.

When it is not necessary to make a decision, never look back.

You talk to yourself because you trust your instincts.

When ideas fail, panic productively.

It is easier to be gigantic than to get a good night's sleep.

By the time you've made it, you can't imagine the smell.

Never trust anyone who chews everything thirty-two times.

Men who never get carried away understand more than you can explain.

If you aren't fired with enthusiasm, forgive and forget.

Victory goes to the player who makes strange things happen.

Of all noises, you can never guard against silence.

Show me a hero, but keep your fingers crossed.

Middle age is when everything has two sides.

The advantage of emotions is that everybody thinks differently.

If people don't want to come out to the ballpark, proceed as if you're not afraid.

If you look like your passport photo, don't pick your scabs.

After three days, do it big or stay in bed.

After all is said and done, dirt is not dirt.

In the end, ride the big waves.

Give a man a free hand and he'll read between the lines.

He who hesitates stops the busywork.

You don't know anything about a woman until there are mice.

No matter how old a mother is, if it tastes awful, you'd better clean your plate.

Having children isn't the whistle that pulls the train.

If you think education is expensive, contribute something to your culture.

Education is the process of spending time with clever people.

Beware of the man who does not move forward in the direction of your convictions.

The worst thing about some men is within everyone's grasp.

Defeat is worse than death because birds sing after a storm.

A lady is one who scratches where it itches.

If you become a star, it is hard to carry a full cup evenly.

Nothing succeeds like cutting your losses.

If you live in New York, you must be moved.

If you have a job without aggravations, don't be a rubber stamp.

The trouble with the rat race is it does not work.

Whoever said money can't buy happiness has secret parts to explore.

Behind every great fortune, there's a tranquilizer with no side effects.

The richer your friends, the greater the confusion.

If women didn't exist, how would men know just how insignificant they really are?

The wages of sin open every door.

If you look good and dress well, forget the feelings and rights of other people.

War is a series of catastrophes littered with sloppy analysis.

You can no more win a war than live within your income.

Start slow and always put off till tomorrow what you shouldn't do at all.

Never get into fights with ugly people, because even a monkey will fall from a tree sometimes.

Never miss a good chance to walk around ladders.

The best way to keep one's word is to apologize liberally.

It's all right letting yourself go as long as you always keep your spurs on.

When walking through a melon patch, patriotism is not enough.

Sometimes a fool is wise enough to be himself.

Good advice will look better in the morning.

When it comes to foreign food, be grateful that God doesn't answer all your prayers.

Life is too short to eat smaller portions.

No man is lonely while living dangerously.

The trouble with life in the fast lane is that a mob has more heads than brains.

The less things change, excuses fool no one.

If you can see the light at the end of the tunnel, don't get attached to things.

When you talk to God, try not to nag.

When dealing with the insane, a dove has no place amongst the crows.

A well-written life is great medicine.

The man who reads nothing at all is better educated than the man who turns up his trousers before he gets to the brook.

If you can't annoy somebody, be grateful for what you have learned.

When in doubt, keep your shirt on.

Anything that is too stupid to be spoken is par for the course.

No sane man will listen to silence.

A critic is a man who takes pandering to a whole new level.

Hollywood is a place where prevention is the best cure.

If you want to make it in show business, don't compare your present lover to the past ones.

Television has proved that you cannot hang everything on one nail.

Man is the only animal that can remain on friendly terms with obeying the speed limit.

Never go to a doctor who reflects daily on the uncertainty of life.

Before undergoing a surgical operation, wait your turn.

Show me a sane man and I will give generously.

If it were not for the government, every day can be extraordinary.

To be content, four hands can do more than two.

It's better to be wanted for murder than become centered in the flow of your life.

If you tell the truth, you choose the lesser of two evils.

It is easier to get permission than count your change.

Even if you're on the right track, avoid the redundant.

People who think they know everything try not to leave words unsaid and deeds undone.

When the going gets tough, children are better observers than adults.

Modern art is what happens when everyone lays a burden on the willing horse.

A life spent making mistakes comes from within.

Friends may come and go, but keep your desk neat.

When down in the mouth, leave your shoes at the front door.

Some people are like popular songs that invite future injuries if you revive the past ones.

God helps those who read between the lines.

Nothing is more conducive to peace of mind than returning all phone calls.

Never accept an invitation from a stranger unless you constantly readjust to your surroundings.

If it weren't for the last minute, you probably wouldn't ever do well.

It is easier to forgive an enemy than turn off the TV.

You are no bigger than the cream of the crop.

We are what we feed our passions.

You can get more with a kind word than a good pillow.

Remember that a kiss on the ass never comes too late.

Nothing is more intolerable than viewing reality from a distance.

Good breeding consists of spending your years ripening instead of rotting.

Charm is a way of getting to yes without maintaining hope.

We are all born charming, fresh, and asking people for things they cannot give us.

Distrust any enterprise that sets your teeth on edge.

It is more fun contemplating somebody else's navel than thinking in clear thoughts.

The difference between pornography and erotica is finding meaning in leisure.

Never play leapfrog with the powers that be.

Of all the tame beasts, noble gestures are as difficult as they are rare.

The happiest time in any man's life is mixture of reality, dreams, and humor.

Never lend your car to anyone to who makes life exciting.

The best revenge is developing your own rituals.

Always be smarter than the people who will believe anything if you whisper it.

The reason American cities are prosperous is part of human nature.

The only way to succeed is to take the dare.

A man can't get rich if scrambled eggs cannot be unscrambled.

Never invest in anything that is easier said than done.

Economists are people who work with numbers but leave a good impression on people.

The secret of staying young is thinking in an unusual way.

No matter how cynical you get, double your joy by sharing it with a friend.

Ignorance is taking the focus off yourself.

Doing a thing well is intellectual back-scratching.

Happiness is an uncertain voyage.

An evil mind teaches us to be less harsh with ourselves.

A thing worth having is next to godliness.

Living with a conscience is the greatest mystery.

In order to preserve your self-respect, take the money and run.

The price of purity is an excuse for not enjoying the present.

A bore is someone who will fall from a tree sometimes.

A louse in the cabbage is better than imagining that everyone is enlightened.

Eating an artichoke is like respecting other people's privacy.

Part of the secret of success in life is eating inspiring foods.

If you want to look young and thin, never resort to personal abuse.

To reduce stress, applying a philosophy is more important than being able to explain it.

Never give a party if you meet adversity with hope.

Never mistake endurance for being consistent.

Nothing spoils a good party like asking philosophical questions.

For a single woman, silence must be as comfortable as conversation.

The best thing about a cocktail party is everybody wants a little cheap attention once in a while.

Sometimes too much to drink narrows your focus.

Like a camel, we can grow in spite of our pain or, perhaps, in response to it.

A gentleman is a man who needs fertilizer in which to grow.

Show me a good loser and conduct yourself with dignity.

If you are going to America, cope calmly to achieve inner serenity.

There is nothing more exhilarating than calling attention to other people's mistakes.

Under certain circumstances, everything hurts.

The trouble with born-again Christians is that common sense is rarely common.

It is better to know some of the questions than show respect for others' time.

It is only possible to live happily ever after if there is no defect except from within.

Dying is one of the few things that will let your character speak for you.

When you don't have any money, the pores of the mind should be left open to all impressions.

The difference between genius and stupidity is that it takes one to know one.

The only reason some people get lost in thought is when nobody's going to stop them.

To love oneself is the last refuse of scoundrels.

When turkeys mate, do your Christmas shopping early.

Tell the truth and purge unneeded information.

When the cat and mouse agree, toss a coin in a wishing well.

Nobody has ever bet enough on the second time around.

It is morally wrong to be a good loser.

It is sometimes expedient to believe in what you are doing.

There is nothing so absurd as when you imagine yourself in the other person's shoes.

Patriotism is the willingness to avoid melodramatic reactions.

The government that robs Peter to pay Paul can't get wool from a frog.

In literature as in love, do not make loon soup.

The man who doesn't read good books usually suspects others of evil.

Even though a number of people have tried, don't eat before you set the table.

Never trust a man unless you can do anything in your dreams.

When men are pure, it is always Judas who writes the biography.

Until you walk a mile in another man's shoes, bring your cooking to an art form.

A man has missed something if he has never collected hotel shampoo bottles.

In any electrical circuit, it works better if you plug it in.

A man can wear a hat for years without laughing at inappropriate times.

We all have the strength to let some things remain a mystery.

There is no sweeter sound than bagpipes in a case.

It takes a great man to get rid of all the extras.

One of the symptoms of an approaching nervous breakdown is that you find fault with what you do not understand.

A little inaccuracy sometimes adds purpose to life.

There is nothing in the world so enjoyable as not getting off the merry-go-round before it stops.

A good deed never lasts forever.

Man is not the only animal that tastes more or less like chicken.

You can't steal second base and allow suckers to keep their money.

When something good happens, give a man a fish.

If you want an audience, make fun of other people.

Nothing is said that avoids electronic overload.

Talk is cheap because possibilities are infinite.

The race may not be to the swift nor victory to the strong, but even logic has its limits.

A liberated woman is one who takes a leap of faith.

If you haven't got anything nice to say about anybody, intuition is often as important as the facts.

Nature has given us two ears to learn to spell.

Absence makes the heart the best icebreaker.

The biggest sin is criticizing a gift.

The higher the buildings, the more you should expect to suffer evil.

Nothing is illegal if the things that hurt instruct.

The future isn't for everyone.

Forgive your enemies, but set television rules.

There is no pleasure in being aware of what you are worried about and why.

Hope is the feeling you have that timing is everything.

They say you can't do it, but not before they are hanged.

It can be great fun to count your blessings.

He who hesitates is not only lost but can't even fish in a herring barrel.

Section 2

To Add Stress to Your Life, Meditate on These

Time is nature's way of making you sell yourself short.

Reality is a crutch for people who hang loose.

The best way to lose weight is to live frugally.

If a thing cannot be fitted into something smaller than itself, do more with less.

The importance of the man and his job does not last forever.

The more unworkable the urban plan, the higher the buildings.

Those who don't study the past pursue more than just pleasure.

Never leave hold of what you've got until you compose yourself.

If you want to understand your government, pay off your mortgage early if possible.

People will believe anything if you give to charity.

A parade should have some things you never get used to.

If you're confident after you've finished an exam, remember that a little uncertainty is good.

If builders built buildings the way programmers wrote programs, mistakes would become food for a new invention.

Nothing is impossible for the man who doesn't go to bed angry.

If you're already in a hole, moral victories don't count.

Associate with well-mannered persons and do not get off the ladder before you reach the ground.

Run with decent folk and make a wish list.

The intelligence of a discussion diminishes at the moment of truth.

In any human enterprise, some things look better from a distance.

A man without religion is like a fish without lemon.

When stupidity is a sufficient explanation, face the music.

By definition, when you are investigating the unknown, a roving eye misses opportunities.

If an organization carries the word "united" in its name, master fear.

If you can't convince them, don't kill a fly with a hatchet.

No matter how many rooms there are in the motel, lawyers could be an important source of protein.

The number of errors made is better than no meat at all.

When you're sure you're right, tell the truth and run.

In order to make a person covet a thing, always look for what others overlook.

Friends may come and go, but obscurity is forever.

Those who expect the biggest tips sing after a storm.

If you see a man approaching you with the obvious intent of doing good, take time to turn yourself around.

The more efficient we get, the more imperfections can make things perfect.

If you want a track team to win the high jump, expect adversity.

For every credibility gap, philosophers discover more than they solve.

He who shouts the loudest catches the largest fish.

The best way to not die is to make the first move.

Under any conditions, anywhere, whatever you are doing, you still have a lot to learn.

If a political candidate chooses to go into specifics on a program, learn to ignore the inconsequential.

If it can be understood, expect great challenges.

The chief cause of having problems is signing up for things you hate to do.

The effectiveness of a politician is a function of how well she makes a spectacle of herself.

The length of a meeting rises by playing second fiddle.

Build a system that even a fool can use, and make up your own instructions for life.

In order to discover anything, don't believe everything you read.

If you wish to make an improved product, separate yourself from the mob.

If you can't measure output, every day can be extraordinary.

Laziness begins every morning when you wake up.

If it works, try not to bark up the wrong tree.

In a crisis that forces a choice to be made among alternative courses of action, wait your turn.

The easiest way to find something lost around the house is to fight for just causes.

In any organization, every path has a puddle.

In dealing with the press, never despair.

In a restaurant with seats that are close to each other, keep the wolf from the door.

Fanaticism consists of redoubling your efforts to expect adversity.

The wider any culture is spread, absurdity appears to be more the rule than the exception.

If the people of a democracy are allowed to do so, they regard all things as straw dogs.

Anything that begins well will eventually kill you.

Whatever hits the fan, there are plenty of other fish in the sea.

If an apparently severe problem manifests itself, do not think small.

When in doubt, do not count too much on friends.

When polls are in your favor, sometimes your opinion needs to be altered.

If you're coasting, forget blunders and absurdities as soon as you can.

History shows that money will open your eyes.

The solution to a problem changes in the present moment.

If it works well, keep the ball rolling.

If the experiment works, face the consequences of your actions.

If you break a cup or plate, get rid of everything that isn't good for you.

When you don't know what to do, listen to what your body says.

All things being equal, things could be worse.

Anything good is either illegal, immoral, or will have big ears.

For the first time in history, there is a lid for every pot.

If it tastes good, don't let the tail wag the dog.

A bird in the hand pays to believe in miracles.

If two wrongs don't make a right, share the remote control.

All other things being equal, one leg cannot dance alone.

If you can keep your head when others around you are losing theirs, stay ahead of the pack.

In an underdeveloped country, don't play with your food.

No man is lonely while living his ideals.

If the newspapers of a country are filled with good news, be prepared for emergencies.

If you don't say it, play it close to the vest.

Where you stand depends on your listening to your feelings.

Anything left over today will bring your cooking to an art form.

For every human problem, selective distrust is the parent of security.

No matter which train you are waiting for, row away from the rocks.

When it's not needed, there's always room for improvement.

The longer the title, always leave them wanting more.

No matter what happens, the ripest fruit falls first.

If facts do not conform to the theory, don't shout "Dinner!" until you have your knife in the loaf.

When properly administered, accidents happen.

If it jams, do not push your luck.

Just when you get really good at something, don't provoke the rage of a patient man.

The longer ahead you plan a special event, the more you need to remember that very few things happen at the right time.

If you just try long enough and hard enough, it is impossible to keep up.

People will buy anything that finds solutions to life's puzzles.

If a thing is done wrong often enough, you'll be happy.

No matter where you stand, carry spares.

The bigger the man, the more you have to accommodate him.

If things were left to chance, the majority is often wrong.

When the law is against you, remember that even monkeys fall out of trees.

Being frustrated is disagreeable, but don't live with the brakes on.

The sun goes down just when you need it.

If you want to kill any idea in the world today, look for the silver lining.

If you have always done it that way, know what you are doing.

In the fight between you and the world, never mistake endurance for hospitality.

The man who can smile when things go wrong should fear the truth.

Once the erosion of power begins, remain calm.

No matter how many times you've had it, if it's offered, take it, because some problems baffle even the wisest people.

In order to get a loan, share your favorite recipes.

When your opponent is down, get it in writing.

The higher a monkey climbs, understanding more is not necessarily better.

For a single woman, true relaxation is an art.

In order to preserve your self-respect, take time to turn yourself around.

Give a woman an inch and eventually everything gets done.

Opera is when a guy gets stabbed in the back and there is no defect except from within.

Today if something is not worth saying, big lies are usually more believable than small ones.

Critics are to authors what shock absorbers are to automobiles.

Under certain circumstances, we must pay attention.

The trouble with born-again Christians is that God doesn't answer all our prayers.

It is better to know some of the questions than to live another life.

It is only possible to live happily ever after if you do not kiss and tell.

Life is like an overlong drama through which every tale can be told in a different way.

The best way to get praise is reinvent yourself.

To love oneself is to decide on an inner discipline that protects oneself.

Reality is a crutch for people who profit from your mistakes.

Anyone who eats three meals a day should understand that you never send a dog to deliver a steak.

Too err is human, to forgive is a wish turned upward.

The only normal people are those who hesitate for a good reason.

A hypocrite is a person who takes the road less traveled.

The two hardest things to handle in life are waiting and hoping.

There is no human problem that could not be solved if you soften your most stubborn positions.

It is not the bait that lures, so think in clear thoughts.

Given enough time, it is later than you think.

The less there is between you and the environment, the more likely your unknown territory may be someone else's home.

The less you enjoy serving on committees, buy in bulk.

Anything hit with a big enough hammer cannot keep a good man down.

To build something that endures, repeat directions back to the person who gives them to you.

Once the erosion of power begins, no one else will do it for you.

No matter how many times you've had it, things could be worse.

Section 3

Advice for Confusing Loved Ones

The happiest liaisons are guided by your dreams.

A relationship is what happens between two people who love the unknown.

The only time a woman succeeds in changing a man is when not everything can be defined.

One good thing about being a man is that men never leave home without a sense of humor.

Few things are harder to put up with than marrying for money.

Better to have loved and lost than take responsibility for your life.

It is dangerous to be sincere, unless you marry someone who has more troubles than you.

There are very few people who kiss slowly.

The trouble with living in sin is that debt is a hard taskmaster.

Marriage is really tough because life is a balancing act.

Alimony is jury-rigged.

One reason people get divorced is that the best successes come from disappointments.

For a relationship to succeed, don't spit in the wind.

The fire of a past love is rarely understood.

Whatever women do, surround yourself with things that make you smile.

If you think God wanted sex to be fun, expect adversity.

A man can't be too careful in making love.

Never let a domestic quarrel take the scenic route.

The bigger they come, the more you need to think hard about who you marry.

For a relationship to succeed, always keep your spurs on.

If love is blind, make an honest woman of her.

If you have a garden and a library, make love when you can.

When you love someone, know when enough is enough.

A lover without indiscretion looks for the favorable parts.

The most important thing in a relationship between a man and woman is don't over schedule.

Section 4

Thoughts to Occupy Your Mind during a Boring Sermon

When it's not needed, ignorance is the enemy of art.

No matter which train you are waiting for, don't deceive yourself.

For every human problem, dramatize your ideas.

When they want it in a rush, always leave a room gracefully.

Where you stand depends on not getting in the way of your own success.

Unless you put your money to work for you, make a secret wish.

You can't tell how deep a puddle is until you pay your bills on time.

Anything left over today unites your mind and body.

No man is lonely while crying in the wilderness.

Coolness comes naturally to a gay lothario.

If you don't say it, suffer fools gladly.

Whatever you want to do, predict dire consequences.

Persons disagreeing with your facts are food for thought.

The more complex the idea or technology, the more you can depend on someone else.

In any collection of data, not everything can be put in order.

If things can go wrong, find any port in a storm.

If only one parking space is available, don't let anyone intimidate you.

When you have accumulated sufficient knowledge to get by, cut yourself some slack.

The less people know about how sausages and laws are made, the easier it is for them to forget the failures of others very quickly.

When you say that you agree to a thing in principle, do not end up where you do not think you belong.

In any given row, the people with seats on the aisle give snakes the right of way.

Marriages are like union contracts: six weeks after the fact, one cannot feel happiness all of the time.

If you have a bunch of clowns, there is a gullibility gap.

If everything seems to be coming your way, see more than what your eyes show you.

A really good fair must treat all religious matters reverently.

He who tries to pick all the flowers knows what will happen to him during the day.

If you think it's tough now, give more than you planned to.

In the arms of Morpheus, a man must be present when he is being shaved.

When in doubt, think of something funny.

No matter what year it is, there is safety in numbers.

You should always judge a man by enduring patiently that which cannot be avoided.

If you are happy where you are, a country in which there is no free lunch is no longer a free country.

It's not the time you put in, it's that some people need more than others.

Don't put off until tomorrow what is essential in life.

To get things done, say what will convince, not what you believe.

Let bravery be your choice, but support the consensus.

When you hit the stars with your head, veto other options.

You don't need a necktie if you can predict dire consequences.

If you turn the other cheek, argue timing, not substance.

Don't agonize—leak what you don't like.

If things stay the same, most of our future lies ahead of us.

If you doubt an action is just, don't tell likely opponents about a good thing.

If worst comes to worst, don't fight the consensus.

If you're there before it's over, step on it.

If somebody will fund it, spiritual travel has many routes.

When eating an elephant, don't bite off more than you can chew.

When working toward the solution is a problem, go full circle.

When the plane you are on is late, that's the way the cookie crumbles.

The best way to get praise is to live happily ever after on a day-to-day basis.

No matter in which direction you start, look over your shoulder now and then to be sure someone's following you.

If it moves, you must be using the wrong equipment.

Putting all your eggs in one basket is not evidence of divine guidance.

When your ship comes in, it's always the wrong time of the month.

When there are two conflicting versions of a story, it's all about how you look at it.

When all is said and done, everything needs a little oil now and then.

If you will just sit still, it does not matter if you fall down.

When working around the house, wear two hats.

On a beautiful day, cut the mustard.

The more ridiculous the belief system, the more you can read something into it.

When you're up to your nose, predict dire consequences.

If you aren't cute, ignorance is no excuse.

The moment you have worked out an answer, lay it on with a trowel.

If there is an opportunity to make a mistake, gird up your loins.

A falling body paves the way.

There is nothing more exhilarating than to be shot at when veering toward respectability.

If it can be borrowed and it can be broken, stop the music.

When your ship comes in, you will borrow it and you will break it.

If you want your name spelled wrong, burn your bridges behind you.

Understand that when you eat meat, certain things shouldn't be moved … but will be.

Under current practices, most discoveries are by error.

When one is mindful of one's distance from home, you always find something the last place you look.

In any household, beggars can't be choosers.

If an experiment works, jump for joy.

Reputation is like cake, even in the wrong denomination.

When things are going well, the innocent bystander often gets beaten up.

When the product is destined to fail, play musical chairs.

If not controlled, spiritual travel has many routes.

At some time in the life cycle of virtually every organization, everything can be looked at from a different view.

Praise is only worthwhile when you can offend them with substance.

As the economy gets better, mistakes turn into expertise.

Once a struggle is grasped, everything else gets worse.

The more directives you issue to solve a problem, the more there is bound to be contention.

After the long slumber of ignorance, the worse it gets.

The road to hell is paved with thinly sliced cabbage.

It is morally wrong to wait for the right moment.

In matters of dispute, make your problem their problem.

If your next pot of chili tastes better, predict dire consequences.

It is always darkest just before you transform your data set.

The only way to discover the limits of the possible is to stoop if the roof is low.

When in doubt, nothing is worth doing.

Better to display your ugliness than be a slave to your past.

If at first you don't succeed, you have to be prepared for people throwing bottles at you.

If a program is useful, take it with a grain of salt.

Whenever one word or letter can change the entire meaning of a sentence, read something into it.

In any decision, silence is sometimes the best answer.

When more and more people are thrown out of work, go against the grain.

If you can't measure it, create the illusion of a crisis in the hope it will be acted on.

The bigger they come, the harder they fall—as long as one hand washes the other.

Those with the best advice always carry identification.

If you bite the hand that feeds you, own a big, mean Doberman.

To get action out of management, a good lather is half the shave.

Food that tastes the best opens the floodgates.

If you don't know what your program is supposed to do, pull a rabbit out of your hat.

When people have a job to do, particularly a vital but difficult one, a little ignorance can go a long way.

If a taxpayer thinks he can cheat safely, it will be a blessing to the state.

To beat the bureaucracy, have two guys come through the door with guns.

When in doubt, pack light.

In a hierarchical organization, everyone is selling something.

If you have too many problems, pour oil on troubled waters.

The only things that evolve by themselves in an organization are on tenterhooks.

One of the lessons of history is to keep the pot boiling.

Before a party or a trip, don't waste time grieving over past mistakes.

If on an actuarial basis there is a fifty-fifty chance that something will go wrong, you'll get run over if you just sit there.

Anyone nitpicking enough to write a letter of correction to an editor is only boring to boring people.

The first rule of intelligent tinkering is don't ask the barber whether you need a haircut.

That which we call sin in others will set you free.

He that is full of himself is experiment for us.

The larger the project or job, the more you drink because you want to, not because you have to.

If you think the problem is bad now, go confidently in the directions of your dreams.

If anything else is permanent, you can't take it with you.

With each step taken, there will be someone going slower than you want to go.

In this world, you are as good as your genes.

Don't consent to absolutes when nothing is certain but death and taxes.

When our friends get into power, we should always leave something to wish for.

On the theory that one should never take anything for granted, never say never.

By and large, incompetents often hire able assistants.

At a bargain sale, seeking revenge prevents the wound from healing.

If one knows what the task is, and there is a time limit allowed for the completion of the task, then make the best of a bad situation.

Starting to do something is the hardest part of doing something, and one cannot guess how much it will cost.

If the time and the resources are clearly defined, the middle will fold up.

If there isn't a law, do not think only in absolutes.

When it is not necessary to make a decision, divide and conquer.

Give him an inch and count to ten before you get angry.

He is prudent who is patient, but he'll screw you.

Necessity is the mother of altering your attitudes.

What goes in is more important than anything else.

He who sees only half the problem enters into the chivalrous task of trying to correct a popular error.

One man's junk is always hidden in the most unlikely places.

Ten thousand years from now, outer space will still not be a place for a person of breeding.

Important things that are supposed to happen get in the way of doing what's right.

Don't be humble, especially when people are looking.

He who lives by the crystal ball goes with the odds.

If the facts don't conform to the theory, you can eventually accomplish anything.

All important truths must be disposed of.

If you're so smart, take the scenic route.

A panic is food for thought.

If anything can go wrong with an experiment, keep your mouth closed.

No matter what occurs, the tire is only flat on the bottom.

In any collection of data, it is harder to live with fewer rules than with many.

If a string has one end, keep several irons in the fire.

If the probability of success is not almost one, don't play with your food.

Once things have happened, be prepared for emergencies.

He who gums up the works shall not be disappointed.

If you push something hard enough, you get the most of what you need the least.

What goes in is the best way to accomplish things.

Anyone who says he isn't going to resign four times cannot follow two paths.

If you want to make an enemy, be virtuous.

The great challenge of life is to do someone a favor.

Whatever isn't forbidden is usually available to the seeker.

If there's no reason why something shouldn't exist, there's always delusion.

A town is only as good as whoever has the gold.

Under any system, don't be in a hurry to tie what cannot be untied.

If a research project is not worth doing at all, there is less competition.

If you drop a full can of beer, do not make eye contact with anyone.

If a jury in a criminal trial stays out for more than twenty-four hours, keep your fingers crossed.

If it can break, muddy the water.

Never argue with a man who heaps coals of fire on his head.

If you can't remember it, go climb a tree.

When two people meet to decide how to spend a third person's money, divide the spoils.

Puppy love is one of mankind's oldest illusions.

Until the cows come home, never look a gift horse in the mouth.

Every time you come up with a terrible idea, keep a stiff upper lip.

If there is a wrong thing to say, carry your part of the load.

When one is trying to be elegant and sophisticated, one cannot make an omelet without breaking eggs.

You can lead a horse to water, but a chicken doesn't stop scratching just because the worms are scarce.

In a country as big as the United States, watch the numbers.

Under the most rigorously controlled conditions, some fights are unavoidable.

If it's good, let the punishment fit the crime.

Make the best of a bad bargain, but do not push your luck.

Any event, once it has occurred, arrives every day.

You know you're paranoid when you reach for the high apples first.

The best ideas are like a septic tank: don't just grab the first thing that comes along.

Given enough time, it is always darkest before dawn.

The difference between genius and stupidity is that victory goes to the competitor who makes the next-to-last mistake.

At any given moment, always store beer in a dark place.

In an underdeveloped country, when you are absent, never try to out-stubborn a cat.

Observe the speed limit, and always run a yellow light.

If you want things to stay the same, get a committee working on it.

In the end, a disagreeable task is its own reward.

If things were left to chance, all times would be the good times.

Those who have the shortest distance to travel to a meeting don't tolerate foul language.

When the law is against you, always keep your spurs on.

If a thing is done wrong often enough, then every day is filled with joy.

No matter where you stand, the real disasters in life begin when you get what you want.

The bigger the man, the more he'll avoid brushing bodies.

People will buy anything that's good for nothing.

If it jams, take advice from those you admire.

If it breaks, you are your own example.

If someone can do it, no good deed goes unpunished.

When properly administered, most lies begin as the truth.

Never buy anything simply because you may not get a second chance.

In matters of grave importance, a little bait catches a large fish.

When in Rome, you will always find some Eskimo ready to instruct the Congolese on how to cope with heat waves.

A celebrity is the harp of your soul.

The fellow who laughs last makes the best of a bad situation.

When you are in trouble, avoid electronic overload.

The penalty for success is keeping the home fire burning.

Jogging is for people who don't blame others.

Good taste is better than supporting candidates you believe in.

Your friend is the man who does not try to fix your life all at once.

The trouble with being in the rat race is that you are here now.

A man who moralizes is innocent until proven guilty.

All beginnings cannot take the place of neglect.

If you obey all the rules, play it cool.

Moral indignation is stretching your boundaries.

To keep an organization young and fit, stay foolish.

Good manners involve the art of playing both ends against the middle.

It is better to suffer injustice than take a reference from a clergyman.

Don't wear a hat when the wisest mind has something yet to learn.

A problem has genius, power, and magic in it.

A stitch in time is a penny earned.

You can't teach an old dog to keep an untroubled spirit.

A penny saved is the enemy of creativity.

Don't count your chickens when the tide goes out.

Never give a sucker the same weapons of reason that arm you against the present.

It takes one to enjoy every sandwich.

One rotten apple is bad for the reputation.

If God had wanted man to fly, you should not be in the stock market.

The shortest distance between two points is negotiable.

It never hurts to add insult to injury.

Wisdom often consists of knowing when to rock the boat.

Don't get caught with your pants down, unless they are not necessary to the task at hand.

Only the strong add insult to injury.

If you can't do the time, share the spotlight whenever possible.

When life hands you a lemon, welcome the possibilities.

Loose lips fall by the wayside.

An ounce of prevention is here, there, and everywhere.

Haste makes sour grapes.

It takes two to keep expectations in check.

The quickest way to a man's heart is neither here nor there.

One hand washes a piece of the action.

There's no such thing as far from the madding crowd.

If the shoe fits, be careful what you say.

Let sleeping dogs fly by night.

Keep your pants on when you are drunk.

If you have to ask the price, you will not find what is beyond your hopes.

If you're about to get into a fight, mind your p's and q's.

According to Hoyle, actions speak louder than words.

Ours is not to reason why, but if you say that there are 425 elephants in the sky, people will probably believe you.

If you're going to be crazy, you have an ace in the hole.

The person who does not know himself is afraid of his own shadow.

It is difficult to show moderation when all's fair in love and war.

He who looks behind will never get ants in his pants.

As every schoolboy knows, don't squat with your spurs on.

Better to limp along the right road than to speed on as the crow flies.

Every person has a fatal flaw at his fingertips.

Surround yourself with bright, cheerful colors to taste the joy that springs from labor.

As much time should be spent exercising the mind as is spent beating a hasty retreat.

Decisions are easy when beauty is in the eye of the beholder.

Death does not know beauty is only skin deep.

Generalizations are better late than never.

Where large sums of money are involved, the harder they fall.

Birds of a feather don't rock the boat.

If you can't beat 'em, add insult to injury.

To survive you often have to bite off more than you can chew.

If you have the choice between humble and cocky, bite the bullet.

Friends and good manners will bite the dust.

When the going gets tough, bite the hand that feeds you.

If it isn't one thing, it's just cakes and ale.

When all else fails, stay as busy as a cat on a rolling stone.

If facts do not conform to the theory, draw a blank.

No matter what happens, buy properly fitting shoes.

In any group, endure patiently that which cannot be avoided.

If it is generally known what one is supposed to be doing, you lose.

In any given miscalculation, separate the sheep from the goats.

The hottest places in Hell are reserved for good Samaritans.

The only thing necessary for the triumph of evil is to rattle a stick inside a swill bucket.

No matter what side of an argument you are on, anticipation of pleasure and pain is always greater than the reality of it.

The most savage controversies are better late than never.

The man who strikes first has ants in his pants.

When you have no basis for an argument, be obscure clearly.

Every time an artist dies, take a page out of your book.

Art, like morality, can cave in at any time.

Natural ability without education doesn't suffer fools gladly.

In the country of the blind, the one-eyed king does not try to explain everything.

For purposes of action, keep breathing.

When you see a snake, it's every man for himself.

Never forget what a man says to you when you lose.

When the candles are all out, feel free to experiment with new ideas.

Don't jump on a man unless you make others feel appreciated.

Behavioral psychology is the science of "silly question, silly answer."

A man lives by putting some things on the back burner.

A bore is a man who is the companion of drunkenness.

Nothing is interesting if things done cannot be undone.

The business of government is to lead to tentative outcomes.

Section 5

Come, Sit in the Casual Furniture of Your Mind

Over a long period of time, bad deeds weigh more than good deeds.

To be a success in business, do not carry a joke too far.

If the government were as afraid of disturbing the consumer as it is of disturbing business, you would dump your unwanted baggage.

Only in time of peace are there no laws for love.

Censorship, unlike charity, is sometimes beneficial to forget.

Any country that has sexual censorship makes life exciting.

No member of society has the right to let bygones be bygones.

It is impossible for ideas to compete in the marketplace if there is no accounting for taste.

Just because everything is different doesn't mean hope is always just around the corner.

The more the change, the harder they fall.

It's the most unhappy people who make peace with imperfection.

The art of progress is to preserve order amid change and climb into the ring with Freud.

Society can only pursue its normal course by upsetting the applecart.

Man has an unlimited biological capacity to be obscure clearly.

Integrity has no need of a utility infielder.

The happiness of every country depends upon washing dirty laundry in public.

History is distinction without a difference.

As the twig is bent, many are called but few are chosen.

The health of a democratic society may be measured by loose ends.

No man who is in a hurry bites the bullet.

When a subject becomes totally obsolete, every change is a change for the better.

It is a luxury to bite the dust.

The prime purpose of eloquence is to go scot-free.

To say the right thing at the right time, breathe before you speak.

To say what you think will kill the fatted calf.

Conscience is the inner voice that warns us to pack light.

In matters of conscience, plan big.

The only means of conservation is to computerize your grocery list.

The most dangerous thing in the world is to follow nature.

The middle of the road is where you reduce the danger by half.

The Constitution gives every American the inalienable right to not throw stones.

If you think before you speak, be obscure clearly.

Don't talk unless you make sure you punch first.

To speak ill of others stretches your boundaries.

The real art of conversation is knowing on which side your bread is buttered.

Beware of the man who goes to cocktail parties not to drink but to observe nature working.

If you don't say anything, be exact.

A coward is a hero with inner direction giving himself strength.

Bravery is being the only one who is selling something.

If you are brave too often, you lose.

Courage is walking naked through a fairy tale.

If you see, in any given situation, only what everybody else can see, keep the pot boiling.

No matter how old you get, vote with your feet.

If the critics were always right, you would lose.

That which seems the height of absurdity will take care of us.

If you would be a real seeker after truth, go for broke.

An era can be said to end when beggars can't be choosers.

A blunderer is a man who should not throw stones.

If error is corrected every time it is recognized as such, lay it on with a trowel.

The man who makes no mistakes cannot buy class.

An ethical man is one who drinks at least eight glasses of water a day.

Moral indignation is expecting nothing.

If history repeats itself, go along for the ride.

There's one thing more painful than learning from experience, and that is cutting your losses.

The best substitute for experience is to keep your fingers crossed.

When a man blames others for his failures, don't rock the boat.

The difference between failure and success is reinventing your world.

If you cannot get rid of the family skeleton, put a good face on it.

Nothing is so soothing to our self-esteem as biting the hand that feeds us.

As long as the family and the myth of the family have not been destroyed, the proof of the pudding is in the eating.

A fanatic is one who should stew in his own juice.

If we had no faults, we'd all paint masterpieces.

Nothing is so much to be feared as the optimist seeing the doughnut.

Nothing is terrible with vinegar.

It is not death that man should fear, but seeing things for what they really are.

If fifty million people say a foolish thing, comparisons are unfair.

When you're down and out, don't spend your time waiting.

If you are too fortunate, don't blame others.

Instead of loving your enemies, hit 'em where they ain't.

Nothing so fortifies a friendship as a pig in a poke.

With good heredity, the pessimist sees the hole.

The principle mark of genius is to always be pulling a rabbit out of your hat.

In the battle of existence, always cut the deck.

In the republic of mediocrity, doing the right thing is often painful.

When choosing between two evils, don't mumble.

The only thing necessary for the triumph of evil is 20/20 hindsight.

Behind every great man is a good scare.

All happiness depends on reading the directions carefully.

If a man has important work, the world is his oyster.

We can't all be heroes, because doing the right thing is often painful.

In the theatre, there is a big difference between kneeling down and bending over.

When it rains, don't prod the beach pebble.

You have to give a little to discover hidden passions.

Be part of the solution, and always cut the deck.

Don't flaunt your success, but putt for the dough.

What your life turns out to be is water over the dam.

Get the butterflies in your stomach to fly where the sun never shines.

Real men don't outnumber wise people who take no advice.

Choose the lesser of two evils or go home.

Go big or patronize local merchants.

A stitch in time cannot buy class.

When the issue is simple, and everyone understands it, know your limitations.

If you have nothing to do, go along for the ride.

The most wasted of all days is the day when we have to pay the piper.

You snooze, you avoid quarrels.

Since most people have not changed in millennia, a miss is as good as a mile.

Never buy pies before they are made.

Stop feeding your pig in a poke.

Speak softly and win the last battle.

When all else fails, take the cake.

A watched pot should not make one's blood boil.

The only person who can make you feel bad makes other people tick.

Trust your mother, but look at things in a new way.

It is not enough just to exist; you have to carry a big stick.

Don't count your chickens where the sun never shines.

When all else fails, at least be vague.

Fearing death does not make it easier to act constructively.

If you want something done, doing the right thing is often painful.

Give yourself plenty of time to work with what you have.

Do not fear fewer tomorrows, but keep your fingers crossed.

If you want to catch trout, don't buy a pig in a poke.

What the outside world needs is another cock and bull story.

To live a full life, settle old scores.

Our prime purpose in this life is to wing it.

Greatness is only achieved with a wild goose chase.

If you want peace, leave no stone unturned.

A big head means you can bet your bottom dollar.

If you try to sit on two chairs, leave no stone unturned.

In order to have a meaningful life, grasp at straws.

By endurance, you gain rewards and the grapes of wrath.

No man ever got lost straying off the reservation.

There is no substitute for plumbing the depths.

Be happy when you have your heart in your mouth.

You'll never know how strong you are until you are left holding the bag.

Never do by force that which you can do by going around in circles.

You cannot fake foot-in-mouth disease.

Both of your feet must be on the ground before casting your bread upon the waters.

The optimist sees the doughnut, the pessimist calls his bluff.

When you don't know what to do, pile it on.

The more hands, the more the need to read directions carefully.

Too much knowledge is like a red flag to a bull.

If opportunity knocks, go for broke.

Good communities know when enough is enough.

He labors in vain who plumbs the depths.

Strengthen yourself with a pound of flesh.

When you are upset, show a clean pair of heels.

The best way out of difficulty is to beat around the bush.

The less we know, the more we blow off steam.

Don't listen to those who say, "Share and share alike."

Never put your feet in sour grapes.

In an argument, simplify your eating habits.

Personal growth requires a swan song.

Life is so interesting because history is full of dead people.

Don't flaunt the hounds of Hell.

No one goes through life without a half-baked idea.

There is a difference between the way things are and the handwriting on the wall.

The more that's known, the more it's every man for himself.

When you are in a hole, never be afraid to ask for information.

The problem about a good thing is that every man has his price.

A good scare is half the battle.

If you're driving a car, don't close your eyes to meditate.

After things have gone from bad to worse, shoot the bull.

A fool and his money separate the wheat from the chaff.

To err is human, but the possibilities are infinite.

Before you criticize someone, pull out all the stops.

Never, under any circumstances, pay through the nose.

If a pig loses its voice, bring home the bacon.

If you live in a small town, let sleeping dogs lie.

Generally speaking, let the chips fall where they may.

If a mute swears, keep your eyes peeled.

Never slap a man who's jury-rigged.

When a clock is hungry, improve each shining hour.

The only substitute for good manners is ill-gotten gains.

If it weren't for marriage, there would be less forbidden fruit.

A clear conscience is usually a force to be reckoned with.

Never be afraid to flip your lid.

When cheese gets its picture taken, don't cry over spilled milk.

It's lonely at the top, but it's business as usual.

The shortest distance between two points is always wrong.

You're not drunk if you change your toothbrush every three months.

The trouble with life is people are the same all over the world.

Discretion is the best cure.

He who dies with the most toys is unique is his own way.

The problem with the world is wherever you go, there you are.

If you try to fail and you succeed at it, stand behind your decisions.

If a turtle loses its shell, call his bluff.

If a deaf person has to go to court, he'll experience a conspiracy of silence.

The quickest way to find something lost around the house is to wreak havoc.

You never really learn to swear until you have too many irons in the fire.

For every action, pause for enlightenment.

Change is inevitable except when you choose the lesser of two evils.

If quitters never win and winners never quit, take it with a grain of salt.

Where there's a will, a stitch in time saves nine.

By the time a man is old enough to watch his step, he has rocks in his head.

The trouble with being punctual is that a rotten apple spoils the barrel.

Never leave a room quiet as a mouse.

Experience is what you get when no news is good news.

If carrots are so good for the eyes, maintain the status quo.

If you read in the bathroom, make no bones about it.

If you aren't educated, know the ropes.

A day without sunshine is like a lame duck.

Friends may come and go, but let it all hang out.

The light at the end of the tunnel can heal and reconcile relationships.

For every vision, accept the worst.

Fighting for peace is like conquering ignorance.

The secret to success is going with the odds.

If voting can change things, keep the pot boiling.

Talk is cheap because a fool and his money are soon parted.

An expert repairs the roof when too many cooks spoil the broth.

The longer you stand in line, the more you can view it as a sign of potential success.

Opportunity only knocks when you have to ram it down their throats.

Never underestimate the power of listening to all the things you can't hear.

A closed mouth is negotiable.

Life is about taking leaps; on the other hand, no use being a damn fool about it.

Jesus loves you, but eat dessert first.

A penny saved is the most disturbing and challenging confrontation you will ever have.

Once over the hill, don't worry about flies.

Give a man a fish, and he'll delegate.

If you can't be kind, learn all you can.

The only time the world beats a path to your door is when you over-tip waiters and waitresses.

The trouble with being punctual is you tend to see every problem as a nail.

If you can't be kind, throw one heck of a party.

No matter how much you push the envelope, do stupid things faster.

When in doubt, size doesn't mean much.

If you are bored, nature is a great inspiration.

Reality does not blush.

Think big, watch sunrises, and bite your tongue.

The more you depend on someone else, the more you need to know where the exits are located.

Before you can move others, divide and conquer.

When you are in a hole, become what you have to.

Know what you can control and be aware of the anger of a patient man.

Carry on silent conversations with yourself and omit needless words.

Begin all actions with thought, and go with the odds.

If you can't beat 'em, ask philosophical questions.

In every job, some fights are unavoidable.

Do not pet a porcupine unless you live with the consciousness of a poet.

If you want something changed, read between the lines.

When you come to the end of your rope, remember that life is not an emergency.

Count to ten before you go beyond your limitations.

If you do not know something, a good cry can be very therapeutic.

Get rid of all the extras, but remember simplicity can be overdone.

The more things change, the more you should prepare yourself for reality.

He who sows barley can make the mundane seem interesting.

When you see something that needs doing, know when enough is enough.

When all else fails, listen to your mother.

When one must, be comfortable with not knowing.

Seek the truth and never yield to the pressure of the masses.

If you put nothing in your head, keep on trying until you get it right.

Never give up on what you really want to do, and remember that everyone is naked under their clothes.

If you get off track, do not read magazines with more ads than content.

In order to receive, do not play with fire.

It is good practice to look back before you manicure the wilderness.

Don't throw away the old bucket until you drink at least eight glasses of water a day.

In skating over thin ice, no two people think alike.

The optimist puts his pants on one leg at a time; the pessimist sees the hole.

Section 6

If You're Lost, These Won't Help You Get There

When you are afraid of something, you watch the parade.

When in doubt, weed your own garden first.

To live a full life, begin where you are.

To get the full value of joy, play your cards right.

If you know where you are and what you have to do, eat your vegetables.

If you have to whisper it, always leave them wanting more.

If you don't use it, visualize it.

If you want to keep a secret, do not change horses in midstream.

When a storm surrounds you, feel free to experiment with new ideas.

When you open a door, hold your head up high.

Make the first move, and don't wear a hat that has more character than you do.

Thinking too much about the future makes the last chicken the hardest to catch.

By exploring your underlying beliefs, you keep an open mind.

Before you buy shoes, know when it is time to leave.

In order to be happy, switch from autopilot to manual.

If you look hard enough, nothing hurts.

If you know how to live well, don't peek into a cannon.

Each day, live it up.

If you are bored, build a margin of safety.

Make tough decisions, and give thanks for your food.

If you give someone an inch, get someone to pay you for doing it.

In order to feel good, remember that being too sane is a sign of madness.

Bait the hook well, and leave the party on a high note.

If you look good and dress well, floss your teeth.

It's not what we don't know that hurts, it's that the end doesn't always justify the means.

If you aim at nothing, go whole hog.

Always look people in the eye when you buy in bulk.

If you have done it right, you will be cursed.

Ears are not made to shut, but listen to silence.

When you've reached your goal, do not cross the stream to find water.

If you cannot run with the dogs, keep your ancestors alive in your heart.

Unless you can do better, be your own best friend.

When you bring in something new, be on time.

It is easy to perform an act of goodness, but don't attend the auction if you don't have money.

Sometimes by going slower, size doesn't mean much.

After you've worked to get what you want, share your favorite recipes.

If you cannot believe everything will turn out the best, don't walk when others stop.

In difficult situations, there is no such thing as too much style.

It is not how you arrive at the truth, it's how you put a good face on it.

Before healing others, don't air your dirty laundry.

If you know you are going to lose, don't tolerate foul language.

If the shoe fits, emit positive energy.

In literature as in love, do not make loon soup.

If you don't know the answer, always leave them laughing.

You can't teach an old dog to vigilantly practice indifference to external conditions.

If you want to gather honey, build a margin of safety.

The faster you get information, the more being able to forget is as important as being able to remember.

If you would not write it and sign it, don't bore people with dramatic stories of your exploits.

In times of great stress and adversity, share the remote control.

Real men don't pay the piper.

In a battle, know when to be quiet.

When speaking in public, plumb the depths.

If someone throws you a ball, don't proselytize.

If you miss the first buttonhole, do it with style.

In every victory, be careful who you laugh at.

If you reveal a weakness, know your situation well.

A watched pot gathers no moss.

Half a loaf is better than a formal weapon.

In an orderly house, things may not be what they seem.

Before you buy shoes, consider things from every angle.

If it sounds too good to be true, it's water over the dam.

It never hurts to take the cake.

If you can determine where to begin, you will know you are there.

He who digs a pit for another is in over his head.

From a broken violin, silence is golden.

If nothing else in life gives you pleasure, roam.

Even if you are on the right track, occasionally do something unusual.

If you like yourself, leave the herd and think for yourself.

It is never too late to eat inspiring foods.

If you look at life as an adventure, then don't change what you are doing.

There is no accounting for losing an illusion.

To avoid risks, recognize mere appearances for what they are.

As you make your bed, build a margin of safety.

When your time has come, don't get caught with your pants down.

You cannot know too much, but measure your feet.

If the conversation around you is decaying, use the right words.

The more you put into a thing, it is what you do not become that hurts.

If things do not feel right, always listen to the other side.

If you have an important point to make, do not carry a joke too far.

If you can't dazzle them with brilliance, share the credit.

Don't underestimate the value of danger signals.

Where large sums of money are involved, don't approach a horse from the rear.

Take time to deliberate, but evolution may pass you by.

In all forms of strategy, don't count on miracles.

If you're about to get into a fight, sometimes it is wise to withdraw and regroup.

In whatever you are doing, answer the easy questions first.

If people don't occasionally walk away from you shaking their heads, take a moment to meditate.

When a door is hard to open, never assume.

If two friends ask you to be judge in a dispute, never answer a hypothetical question.

When you get to the end of your rope, step to the music you hear.

If you can't change your fate, narrow your focus.

If you are squeamish, set a good example.

Instead of loving your enemies, be concerned with escaping safely.

If you do not fear death, there's always delusion.

Just because it's automatic, understand what guides you.

If you look for the bad in life, knowing your faults is a strength.

If you kick a stone in anger, keep your overhead low.

Once a guy starts wearing silk pajamas, diversify your investments.

If you say that elephants are flying in the sky, reinvent your world.

Before you can steal fire from the gods, know what you are doing.

The important thing is to sit down to the table and beat a dead horse.

If you can possibly avoid it, turn up your trousers before you get to the brook.

When looking at any significant work of art, don't whine.

Smoked carp tastes just as good as smoked salmon when the chickens come home to roost.

The second rule of life is every man has a price.

Confession may be good for the soul, but some things are just easier to say across the remains of a shared meal.

If you are scolded, flattery will get you nowhere.

When you become afraid, do an about-face.

Don't ever talk until you bring a horse to water.

The greatest secrets are par for the course.

If error is corrected whenever it is recognized as such, do it well or not at all.

The time to relax is when you are more connected to the universe.

If you want a place in the sun, get rid of all but two credit cards.

People who put off little things know the true value of time.

Whether the road goes uphill or downhill depends upon being aware of danger signals.

Don't drink and think of ways to improve your life.

If you have to do it every day, always leave them laughing.

It is more difficult to be beautiful than to diversify your investments.

An ending is better than a beginning when you read the instructions.

Make sure the prize you chase is different in your mind than in the mind of others.

All that is known is significantly less than the tip of the iceberg.

To get the full value of joy, sow wild oats.

Pay no attention to things that add insult to injury.

Neither an egg nor an ego is any good until you bear the burden and the heat of the day.

If you can't beat 'em, hog the limelight.

With each step taken, you can bet your bottom dollar.

It takes less time to avoid an accident than to take it with a grain of salt.

An excuse can sometimes be more damaging than killing the goose that lays the golden eggs.

Faith is truth to the person who got up out of the wrong side of the bed.

When you see something that needs doing, burn the candle at both ends.

When we honestly admit our wrongs, we can play a trump card.

If you think about something too much, a picture is worth a thousand words.

The fear of change is usually far worse than an albatross around the neck.

Diplomacy is thinking twice before eating crow.

The grass may be greener on the other side, but blood is thicker than water.

You can feel lonely making hay while the sun shines.

Some things seem easy at first, but doubt is the key to knowledge.

Start at the beginning and view reality from a distance.

An apple a day is the only thing okay to do in excess.

Strong lives are motivated by a fine kettle of fish.

There are no easy answers to unclear questions, questions not properly asked and knowing when to stop.

The bizarre can appear cool if you take the road less traveled.

There is nothing wrong in admitting butter wouldn't melt in her mouth.

Eat your honey, but don't fish in a herring barrel.

If you think too long, do not wade far.

Every time you forgive someone, resist telling others how something should be done.

You can't beat winning, but don't be a martyr.

When life hands you a lemon, don't spit in the wind.

Feelings are useless without answers to your unique set of problems.

When great changes occur in history and where great principles are involved, stupidity has no limits.

Allow your mind to solve problems before you find challenges that test you.

When you are in the wrong, be lovable.

Believe nothing unless you cope calmly to achieve inner serenity.

If you are upset and feel like venting your frustration, be original.

There comes an age in everyone's life when you cannot go far in a rowboat without oars.

A person must lose innocence in order to count on being alive tomorrow.

It is a poor frog who is always greener on the other side of the fence.

Do not criticize your neighbor until you endure patiently that which cannot be avoided.

It is hard to fight an enemy who cooks with tender loving care.

If you think you are free, be open to new suggestions.

If you hurry all the time, less can be more.

Those who bring sunshine to the lives of others know when to be quiet.

People who stay in the middle of the road don't go to bed angry.

Success has a lot to do with outliving your enemies.

Taking a step back from a problem may give you the distance you need in order to think faster than you act.

Beggars should not pay somebody to practice for them.

Section 7

Sino American Mashed Thinking

These are the offspring
of Chinese proverbs and
American wisdom

If you do not put aside your weapons, play fast and loose.

If assumptions are wrong, do not open your clothes to embrace the fire.

When you have faults, anything is possible.

Anytime you wish to demonstrate something, look not for the donkey you are sitting on.

The more heavily a man is supposed to be taxed, the more he should certainly want to fly like a cock.

Everything is more or less like uncarved jade.

There is no victory in trying to make sense of the world.

All men strive to come up for air.

When the wise man becomes a ruler, it's always the partner's fault.

When the first indications of error begin to appear in the state, vote with your feet.

When the enemy asks for truce without warning, thump the tub.

When a thousand homes hear the approach of war, cut no ice.

Great generals never go to a doctor whose office plants have died.

What's worth doing tests the hardiness of a blade of grass.

Today's men are not born to the purple.

The swing of the sword cannot stretch the truth.

One must consider carefully foot-in-mouth disease.

He who has committed no crime by day gilds the lily.

Good and evil both end up in the grave, but a good time was had by all.

Refrain from displaying objects of desire, so hide your light under a bushel.

The foundation of the world lies in going around in circles.

Claiming certainty without corroborating evidence is the lesser of two evils.

When the wise man becomes a ruler, call his bluff.

Only those who are ignorant about government take potluck.

The intelligence of the masses is conspicuous by its absence.

The wise ruler spills the beans.

If the institutions of the former kings are not suitable, like it or lump it.

Only those who have not minds of their own and do not use their own judgment cast pearls before swine.

When a thousand people gather together with no one as a leader, a good time is had by all.

Great generals need not take one for the team.

When a sacred peach waxes green with heaven's dew, read between the lines.

Nothing brings greater misfortune than a millstone around the neck.

Once a struggle is grasped, fly the coop.

To win the battle, see how contently the carp drift through the water.

A big man can afford to lay it on with a trowel.

If we can no longer speak of loyalty to princes, catch as catch can.

An old horse at the trough still eats humble pie.

A hero in his old age never slices the melon.

In death and life, your friends are goody two-shoes.

Reputation is like the devil incarnate.

Although the bird has not taken flight, run with the hares, hunt with the hounds.

How can the swallow understand the aspirations of ships that pass in the night?

He who commits too many sins is a forgone conclusion.

Do not claim to be the disciple of saving grace.

The truly wise man does not hang in there.

If you do only ordinary things, curry favor.

The wise man must think hard before drawing a blank.

Good deeds attract glory, glory attracts fortune, and fortune wears the pants in the house.

The wise man does not seek to influence the eternal triangle.

One who sets his heart on doing good faces the music.

Seek friends who are better than you, not the Boston Brahmin.

Boasts are harder to honor than a green-eyed monster.

It is a disgrace for a gentleman's words to be greater than his last gasp.

It is easier to go up a mountain and catch a tiger than holding a prayer meeting in a sauna.

Elevation of the worthy is kneeling down and bending over.

Praise is only worthwhile when you drag them down to your level.

Do not make the news of you as rare as forty winks.

He who speaks without modesty respects the natives.

Drinking till dazed, you can take your time going around the bases.

He who does evil hands down the last laugh.

When one is mindful of one's distant home, the truth can be very unpopular.

The worthy leader starts the day early and never uses a metaphor or simile.

Unconstructive criticism is like keeping an untroubled spirit.

He who strives after truth doesn't worry about insects in general.

If only good men were appointed to office, it would be a sign that the end is near.

If a light offense is lightly punished, it makes people want to kick you.

Failure lies not in falling down, but in smiling because it happened.

The shining virtue of the sage must gamble everything for love.

One look is worth a jot or tittle.

To catch a tiger's cub, live like a mudfish.

The more laws made, the more you should make sure you tip generously.

Better to display your ugliness than worry about flies.

When you aim at the rat, don't prod the beach rubble.

When a distinguished but elderly scientist states that something is possible, it would not do to speak it to the vulgar crowd.

No matter how often you trade dinner or other invitations with in-laws, a tiger does not take insults from sheep.

A hundred men scrambling to fetch a gourd by cart results in a low priority for repair work.

If you have something to do and you put it off long enough, resign yourself to the morbid love of wine and excessive passion of women.

The more qualified candidates who are available, the more you need to beware a dagger in a smile.

The more time you spend in reporting what you are doing, the more you should spare not the tether if it costs you your cow.

Seek friends who are better than you, not thinly sliced cabbage.

Section 8

All Mashed Chinese, All The Time

These are the pearls of wisdom you could have heard in ancient China after a night of binge drinking.

When the fruit is heavy, the bough is strained; when the bough is strained, catch not lice on the tiger's head.

Even if you are endowed with the sharpest sense of hearing, a sour wind impales the eyes.

He who governs by example is not fit to be deemed a scholar.

The administration of government depends on having bowels of iron.

He is victorious who knows when straight wood does not require the carpenter's tools.

When good is in danger, large chickens don't eat small rice.

You can deprive an army of its commander, but better a fox's fur than the skins of a thousand sheep.

Men, when suffering injustice, stoop if the roof is low.

He who strikes first is like uncarved jade.

When a man's transgressions are great, we must let down our hair and go boating.

When the rabbit is dead, there is no need to ask a fortune teller.

When riding a tiger, the wise man does not stand beneath a collapsing wall.

Those who seek everlasting life on earth must carry with them a cartload of demons.

Among barbarians, look not for the donkey you are sitting on.

When the work of the perfect leader is done well, see how contently the carp drift through the water.

It is not wise for a blind man riding a blind horse at midnight to let another man snore beside his own couch.

Good government is attained when gossip flies and spreads far.

To gain the respect of the people, it is bad luck to kill those who have already surrendered.

Although the rivers and mountains of the world have not changed, toilet facilities are still largely al fresco.

When you see a straight piece of wood, spare not the tether if it costs you your cow.

Keep your mouth shut when cheap meat is bulked with fat.

He who is moved neither by slander that gradually seeps into the mind nor by statements that startle like a wound in the flesh is not perfect, but he is not stupid either.

After the initial cut, a paper tiger is not so fierce.

Poke the flames, and if you bow at all, bow low.

One does not need a lantern when clouds follow the dragon.

To give peace to the Empire and suppress rebellion, do not use firewood to put out a fire.

People are obedient to the ruler who tests the hardiness of a blade of grass.

One should not expect gratitude when dying embers can still start a fire.

By using bronze as a mirror, half an orange tastes as sweet as a whole one.

He who steals a chicken while small will be given to vomiting.

A battering ram can knock down a city wall, but do not stand by a tree stump waiting for a hare.

When the enemy is defeated, rejoice in his misfortunes.

When you are drunk, orchids have a fragrance fit for a king.

Sending untrained recruits into battle is like climbing a tree to look for fish.

The blacker the wok, ding is ding and mao is mao.

To defeat an army, we go buy wine.

With men as with silk, a giant corpse only feeds more vultures.

If the chariot ahead has overturned, do not take the seeds and throw away the melon.

The secret of leading soldiers is like hurling an egg against a rock.

Better for one family to weep than to all look the same without their hair.

When a deer's life is in danger, the caged bird yearns for the forest.

If a horse gives you trouble, go not ahead with nothing in front.

When the birds are dead, there is bound to be contention.

If your deeds displease the people, lay not a corpse at someone else's door.

If anyone wants courage, the petty man will do the exact opposite.

When the men first hear the beat of the war drums, beware an ear laid close to the wall.

In order to live a long time, beat the grass to frighten the snakes.

Since ancient times, a small man is hard on others.

Kingdoms rise and kingdoms fall, but porcelain dogs do not keep watch at night.

When the hot water for the bath is ready, four horses cannot drag it back.

It is difficult not to complain when one is poor, but making an axe handle requires wood cut with an axe.

Even the hardiest plant will not flourish if one arrow scares five boars.

A fish that frees itself from a hook takes two flints to make a fire.

Section 9

A Taste from the Old Country

If you wish to be loved, swim without corks.

Hold your tongue and bear with the hen.

If thou follow thy star, thou have done so unwittingly.

If you wish to learn how to pray, prepare for war.

Once an abbot, an old man is twice a boy.

If it is not true, force a laugh.

He who lives without folly timidly courts denial.

Those who resemble each other shall guard the guards themselves.

He who sings is always on the side of the big battalions.

The sharp scent of the hounds cannot make an orange tree out of a bramble bush.

When there is little bread, virtue is the safest helmet.

With chopped parsley, butter sauce, and lemon juice, tremble before the trumpet.

Everything unknown has its reverse side.